YOU KNOW YOU'RE A CHILD OF THE 1980S WHEN...

CHARLIE ELLIS

summersdale

YOU KNOW YOU'RE A CHILD OF THE 1980s WHEN...

This revised and updated edition copyright © Summersdale Publishers Ltd, 2020
First published in 2016

Text by Mark Leigh, Mike Lepine, Vicky Edwards and Lucy York

Illustrations by Julie Goldsmith; icons © Shutterstock.com

An Hachette UK Company
www.hachette.co.uk

Summersdale Publishers Ltd
Part of Octopus Publishing Group Limited
Carmelite House
50 Victoria Embankment
LONDON
EC4Y 0DZ
UK

www.summersdale.com

Printed and bound in China

ISBN: 978-1-78783-344-9

Substantial discounts on bulk quantities of Summersdale books are available
to corporations, professional associations, and other organizations. For
details contact general enquiries: telephone: +44 (0) 1243 771107 email:
enquiries@summersdale.com.

To...

From...

YOU KNOW YOU'RE A CHILD OF THE 1980s WHEN...

Amstrad and Commodore still say "cutting-edge technology" to you.

You couldn't wait to find out why, thanks to Apple, **1984** wouldn't be like *1984*.

New Romantics aren't the latest page-turners from Mills & Boon.

Opium and **Poison** are substances that hold no fear for you, although death by excessive use of overpowering fragrance is, admittedly, a possibility.

DO YOU REMEMBER...

Charles and Diana's Wedding

Widely considered to be the wedding of the century, millions of us tuned in to watch Prince Charles and Lady Diana Spencer get hitched on July 29, 1981. It seemed such a beautiful fairy story back then…

The Running Man

Showcased by the likes of MC Hammer and Vanilla Ice, the running man dance—which consisted of rowing an invisible boat while running on an imaginary treadmill—was considerably easier than that other breakdancing staple, the headspin.

ARCADES

Weekends were made for spending inside
one of these game-filled treasure troves.
Who needs sunlight when you can bathe
in the artificial glow
of cathode-ray
display
screens,
pinballing
and Donkey-
Konging your
way to glory?

YOU KNOW YOU'RE A CHILD OF THE 1980s WHEN...

It still amazes you that **hairstyles** can be achieved with anything less than an **entire can** of maximum-hold **hairspray**.

You know that **Band Aid** is much, much more than a sticking plaster.

You remember testing the limits of the **phone cord** to get some privacy on a call. No matter how far you got, someone would still be listening in on the **other line**.

Your 12-year-old crushes were **Rob Lowe**, George Michael and the one who is now a bit chubby from **Spandau Ballet**.

QUIZ

1. What was the name of the toy that gave you words to spell via an electronic voice?

2. What were the names of the pastel-colored teddies that we all went crazy for?

3. Name the ugly dolls that took their name from a vegetable?

4. Which doll came in tiny pocket sets?

5 What math aid was Little Professor?

6 Which popular drawing game came onto the market in 1985? (Clue: it's a bit like charades.)

6 Which brand had a schoolhouse as part of its Little People range?

8 A model of which feline-sounding car that featured in a popular TV show was one of the most requested Christmas gifts of the 1980s?

YOU KNOW YOU'RE A CHILD OF THE 1980s WHEN...

You remember being transfixed by the efforts to rescue Baby Jessica from the bottom of a well in Texas.

You still want to go to the High School of Performing Arts and start paying. In sweat.

Whether you were team Pepsi or team Coca-Cola, you knew where your loyalties lay in The Cola Wars.

You still haven't gotten over the discovery of the fact that Darth Vader is Luke Skywalker's father.

DO YOU REMEMBER...

Summer Camp

At summer camp you lived for the day when your care package would arrive. But you lived in fear of the day you would see underwear being run up the flagpole and realize it was yours or being part of whatever spooky tales were passed around the campfire over s'mores.

Techno Disney

In 1982 the Epcot Center at Walt Disney World opened: a showcase of humanity's technological achievements and innovations. It included such delights as World of Motion and Body Wars, a motion simulator that "miniaturized" guests and transported them on a journey inside the human body.

Kellerman's Resort

After watching *Dirty Dancing* at least twice at the movie theater, you longed to time travel to the 1960s for your summer vacation, having the time of your life learning how to shimmy like Swayze and Grey in the Catskill Mountains.

Birthday Parties

The best birthday parties involved bouncy castles, pizza, and a VHS copy of *The Goonies*. If you were lucky, your mom might have baked you a cake, but the best thing was having fun with your friends.

Public Swimming Pool

Yes, they still exist, but back in the 1980s they were THE place to hang out in the summer. Especially as the main reason you went was to stare at the hunky lifeguard you were crushing on.

Hands Across America

In 1986, 6.5 million strangers joined hands to play their part in the fight against hunger and homelessness by joining a continuous human chain that stretched across the States. Even if you weren't there for the event itself, you remember recreating it in the schoolyard.

YOU KNOW YOU'RE
A CHILD OF THE
1980s
WHEN...

You spent every Friday night
with the **Ewing family**.

You still get a craving for
Jell-O Pudding Pops.

Fingerless lace gloves might
make you look like you've been
raiding Great-Aunt Maud's
attic but you happen to think
they look cute, quirky, and
very **"material girl."**

You once sat through six hours
of MTV in the hopes of catching
Duran Duran's **"Rio"** video.

QUIZ

ONLY A CHILD OF THE 1980s WILL KNOW...

1 What was the name of the ThunderCats' furry, red-and-yellow companion?

2 What type of creature was the puppet in *ALF*?

3 Which resourceful TV character could figure his way out of any dangerous situation given a couple of rubber bands, a battery, and a paperclip?

4 What was He-Man's homeland called?

5 What was the name of Danger Mouse's diminutive sidekick?

6 Who did the Fraggles live in fear of?

7 What was the name of Bobby's pet in *Dungeons & Dragons*?

8 What were the two warring alien robot factions in *The Transformers*?

YOU KNOW YOU'RE A CHILD OF THE 1980s WHEN...

It doesn't matter who tries to tell you differently: **Fergie** is not a member of The Black Eyed Peas.

You know EXACTLY
who ya gonna call.

Your parents would have
preferred that you didn't
like the **Beastie Boys.**

If someone talks about
"phoning home," you
immediately want to do
a silly little growly voice
and point your index
finger at the sky.

DO YOU REMEMBER...

New Romantics

Duran Duran, Talking Heads, The Police, Depeche Mode, Culture Club... all part of the New Wave or New Romantic trend ("post-punk," musically speaking). We all longed to play the synth, wear frilly shirts and make-up, and demonstrate our self-expression and coolness.

Hair Metal

It gave us the likes of Bon Jovi, Van Halen, and Poison: rockers with big hair, who made our hearts thump in time to their relentless rhythms; their songs have become some of the most enduringly popular karaoke turns.

HIP-HOP

Hip-hop was new, exciting, and brash, brash, BRASH! Run-DMC, Beastie Boys, Grandmaster Flash—it was all becoming mainstream and, predictably, our parents loathed it. Which made us even more devoted.

YOU KNOW YOU'RE A CHILD OF THE 1980s WHEN...

You got excited when **Gatorade** released their new **"fruit punch"** flavor.

"Whatchoo talkin' 'bout, Willis?" is a phrase that you still use regularly—with gusto.

Saturday mornings were made for watching *Pee-wee's Playhouse*.

You thought that a **gold belcher chain** was a status symbol that was internationally recognized. (You were wrong.)

QUIZ

1. Which George Michael song was the best-selling single of 1988 in the US?

2. Which group had a hit with "You Spin Me Round (Like a Record)" in 1984?

3. Pepsi and who were a SAW act?

4. What did Mel and Kim say they were "never gonna be" in 1987?

5 Which girl band "heard a rumour" in 1987?

6 Who had a hit with "Never Gonna Give You Up"?

7 Which NFL team released the song "Super Bowl Shuffle" in 1985?

8 Which artist wanted to dance with somebody in 1987?

YOU KNOW YOU'RE A CHILD OF THE 1980s WHEN...

Whenever you enter a burger joint you have the urge to bellow **"Where's the beef?"**

You remember when presidents were more interested in **tearing down walls** than building them.

You're still a **Numanoid** at heart.

You dared your little sister to say **"Beetlejuice!"** three times.

Smurf-Berry Crunch

Saturdays wouldn't be Saturdays without a bowl of this berry-flavored cereal, wolfed down while watching the latest episode of *The Smurfs*, of course.

Shell Magic

This sauce, which hardened on ice cream, was the ultimate in pudding paraphernalia. Part-sweet and part-science, the ritual of topping your sundae and watching it solidify was a thrilling experience.

SuperPretzel

The convenience snack that brought the ballpark home. All you needed to do was add a sprinkle of water and salt, put it in the microwave, and ping!—30 seconds later you could tuck into your favorite ballpark snack.

Hubba Bubba

This bubblegum, favored by Wild West cowboys, allowed you to blow big bubbles with no troubles, because it peeled easily off your nose once the bubble inevitably burst, unlike other, stickier brands.

Nerds

These tiny, brightly colored, sugar crystal candies came in duo-compartment boxes, with two flavors per box, packing a punch with every bite.

Reese's Pieces

Every kid went out and bought a giant bag after a boy called Elliot laid a trail of these yellow, orange, and brown peanut butter treats to lure an extra-terrestrial in 1982. The product placement of Reese's Pieces in *E.T.* is still lauded as the most successful in advertising history.

YOU KNOW YOU'RE A CHILD OF THE 1980s WHEN...

You wanted to do the *Gold Run* so badly it hurt...

You regularly remind your friends:
"Let's be careful out there."

You'd still like to float up into the clouds and visit **Care-A-Lot**.

The hole in the **ozone layer** kept you awake at night and made you think guiltily about the three cans of maximum-hold **hairspray** you'd used earlier in the day...

QUIZ

ONLY A CHILD OF THE 1980s WILL KNOW...

1. What did Tim Berners-Lee give the world? (Clue: it's bigger than TV.)

2. In which unforgettable movie did Meg Ryan fake an orgasm in a cafe?

3. Which band kicked off a tour called "Steel Wheels"?

4. What famous barrier was taken down in November 1989?

5 In which square did the Chinese government kill protesting students?

6 Which round-the-clock news network, the first of its kind, was launched in 1980?

7 Which NASA Space Shuttle exploded just 73 seconds after take-off in 1986?

8 What happened on October 19, 1987, also known as Black Monday?

YOU KNOW YOU'RE A CHILD OF THE 1980s WHEN...

Whenever friends go on a **backpacking trip** you remind them to "keep to the road, stay clear of the moors, and **beware of the full moon.**"

No potluck was complete without **spinach dip** in a bread bowl, **tricolor pasta salad**, and **sloppy joes**.

You would have happily spent all day playing **Pac-Man**.

You can't believe you'll never have another birthday party at **The Ground Round**.

Chiffon Scarves

Thanks to artists like Bananarama, Madonna, and Cyndi Lauper, we were raiding thrift stores and our grandma's wardrobes for these perfect hair accessories, which ideally needed to be in the brightest possible shades.

Upturned Collars

"Turn it up" was the advice of fashionistas when it came to collars. Jackets or shirts—both, in fact—this was the way a man about town would rock the 1980s look. Even if it did make you look like you had got dressed in the dark.

WORKOUT CLOTHES

Movies like *Fame* and *Flashdance* helped to make exercise clothes fashionable. Coupled with the advent of the aerobic craze, leotards, headbands, and leg warmers were not just for the gym; there was more Lycra on the streets than could be found in locker rooms.

YOU KNOW YOU'RE A CHILD OF THE 1980s WHEN...

Your party piece is doing the **Rubik's Cube** in less than 40 seconds.

No **make-up bag** has ever surpassed the wonder of your **Caboodle**.

You remember being a bit suspicious of **microwaved** food—you thought it might be **radioactive**.

You wore **neon socks**— odd ones too—thinking they made you look "street."

QUIZ

ONLY A CHILD OF THE 1980s WILL KNOW...

1. From which movie does the term "Bunny Boiler" originate?

2. On which "street" did a nightmare happen?

3. In which weepy did the song "Wind Beneath My Wings" feature?

4. What should you not feed after midnight or get wet?

5. Complete the movie title: Back to the...?

6 Which Star Wars movie was released in June 1983?

7 Who took over the role of James Bond in 1987?

8 Who played Johnny Castle in the movie *Dirty Dancing*?

You believed your older brother when he told you that **Phil Oakey** could only afford half a haircut on his **pop star** salary.

You did all your school **papers by hand** with a fountain pen and you would go to the library to do all your research.

You don't remember **gap years**— people who didn't go straight to college were just doing resits.

You used to wake up to **Lunden and Gibson** or **Pauley and Gumbel,** and Golden Grahams.

DO YOU REMEMBER...

Dangly Earrings

Feathers, beads, diamante, hoops the size of spaceships... Ears were drooping under the weight of big baubles. Still, the more piercings you had, the higher your coolness ranking.

Sweats

Sweats were sweet. Matching sweatshirt and sweatpants—a reimagining of the 1970s tracksuit—was a combo that every well-dressed guy had in his wardrobe. Worn with white running shoes, of course.

Shoulder Pads

Made popular by *Dynasty*, this fashion gave us all trouble getting through narrow doorways. And there was always that really annoying issue arising from machine washing, when the pad got rucked up on the spin cycle and you had to spend ages massaging it back into place.

Magnum P.I. Moustache

In the early 1980s a "Magnum P.I." moustache was the mark of a man. They decreased in popularity as the decade rolled by, as girls disliked the sensation of kissing what felt like a warm Brillo pad.

Puffball Skirts and Poufy Dresses

These abominable styles of the 1980s meant more flounces than an army of divas deprived of their lipgloss. As they tended to be short, you needed good knees, since this was one thing that the ruff 'n' puff style didn't conceal.

Blousy Jackets

Whether in denim or leather, these were all the go. The fact that you looked eight months pregnant was neither here nor there. George Michael wore one and so did all the Duran Duran boys, ergo you wore one. Period.

YOU KNOW YOU'RE
A CHILD OF THE
1980s
WHEN...

You were so annoyed that **Prince Charles** got married, but decided to hold out for Edward instead.

You graffitied a **CND** symbol on your school satchel, along with lyrics to **The Smiths'** "There is a Light that Never Goes Out."

Your bedroom walls were covered with pull-outs of your favorite heartthrobs from *Bop* and *Tiger Beat*.

Your **Filofax** was full of practice signatures for your future life as **Mrs. Adam Ant**.

QUIZ

1 Who played Kevin in *The Wonder Years*?

2 Who played the role of Michelle Tanner in *Full House*?

3 In which city could you find the friendly bar "where everybody knows your name"?

4 Who was the captain of the *USS Enterprise*?

5 Which ensemble provided the music for *Late Night with David Letterman*?

6 Which show starred Bruce Willis and Cybil Shepherd as private detectives?

7 Who played Alex Keaton in the sitcom *Family Ties*?

8 What were the names of the crime-busting duo in *Miami Vice*?

YOU KNOW YOU'RE A CHILD OF THE 1980s WHEN...

Your pristine **Adidas** tracksuit, along with a pair of matching **shell-toe** sneakers, still have pride of place in your wardrobe.

You remember **Paul McCartney** best for being in Wings.

If you didn't have a long **shaggy perm**, you were a social outcast. Same for your partner.

You used to check your wardrobe for signs of **E.T.** before going to bed each night—and were always disappointed when there was no sign of him.

Teenage Mutant Ninja Turtles

Found in a sewer and raised by the kindly ninja Hamato Yoshi, Leonardo, Donatello, Raphael, and Michelangelo—the "heroes in a half-shell"—took Turtle Power to the max. Fighting evil, the battle cry of "Cowabunga, dude!" was heard in playgrounds throughout the decade.

The Inside Story

You learned everything you needed to know about the workings of the human body from this PBS show featuring Slim Goodbody (aka "The Superhero of Health"), played by John Burstein. Burstein wore a white unitard painted with realistic renditions of the inner workings of human anatomy, and often appeared next to giant models of organs.

SHE-RA

Sister show to the ever-popular He-Man, She-Ra was just as enthralling and entertaining. The set up was the same, with a group of quirky allies and a legion of baddies, led by the evil Hordak. The magic-sword swinging and unicorn riding were balanced out by the trademark "moral" delivered by one of the characters at the end of each episode.

YOU KNOW YOU'RE A CHILD OF THE 1980s WHEN...

You took up **keyboard** lessons and begged your parents for a walking piano after watching *Big*.

You remember your friends wearing so many **crucifixes** that you thought there was a massive religious revival.

When it came to drugs, you knew it was best to **"Just say no."**

You once really believed that boys found **puffball skirts** and pixie boots sexy.

QUIZ

1. Which stand-up comedian was *Delirious* in 1983?

2. Which comedian disgraced herself with an inappropriate rendition of "The Star Spangled Banner"?

3. Which sketch comedy show was the birthplace of *The Simpsons*?

4. What was The Diceman's real name?

5 Which charity organization event to raise money for the homeless was founded in 1986 by Bob Zmuda?

6 Which stand-up comedian was crowned Showtime's Funniest Person in America in 1982?

7 Which actor played all of the male roles in *You Can't Do That on Television*?

8 Which comedian released the album *I Have a Pony* in 1985?

YOU KNOW YOU'RE A CHILD OF THE 1980s WHEN...

You fantasized about going on a date with **The Bangles**.

You learned all you needed to
know about self-defense from
watching *The Karate Kid*...

... and all you needed to know
about sex from *Cosmopolitan*.

You asked your careers teacher
about opportunities as a Top
Gun or a Ghostbuster.

DO YOU REMEMBER...

Dallas

Before all the nonsense of Bobby popping out of the shower and Pammie having dreamt a series, *Dallas* in its early days was compulsive viewing: full of pouting beauties, alcoholic moms and evil oil barons.

Airwolf

Michael Knight's talking car, Kitt, was impressive, but Airwolf could fly and blow the hell out of anything! This show was always guaranteed to give thrills, spills, and explosions.

The Dukes of Hazzard

Cousins Bo and Luke Duke had their hands full foiling the crooked plans of corrupt Commissioner Hogg. But even though they often took the law into their own hands, they were "never meaning no harm."

Diff'rent Strokes

Child TV stars were nothing new, but they didn't come much cuter or sassier than little Arnold Jackson (Gary Coleman), with his unforgettable catchphrase, "Whatchoo talkin' 'bout, Willis?"

The Golden Girls

Forget about the vice, this was Miami Nice, with four ladies enjoying their golden years in the house share that every woman secretly hopes she will get to live in when she retires. There was lusty, man-hungry Blanche, outspoken divorcee Dorothy and of course Dorothy's Sicilian mother, Sophia, master of such immortal witty one-liners as "You're old, you sag, get over it."

The A-Team

It was reassuring to think that the A-Team was driving around in their combat van, ready to burst through a brick wall and save the day. No job was too big or too small for these special forces ops gone rogue.

YOU KNOW YOU'RE
A CHILD OF THE
1980s
WHEN...

You remember parties starting with a bottle of **Liebfraumilch**, and ending with the contents regurgitated all over your shoes.

You wished you had **go-go-gadget arms** so that you could reach the treats jar down from the top shelf.

You wished you could own something by **Sergio Tacchini**— or even just be able to spell it.

You understand what's meant by a "**seven-inch single**" and a "**C60 cassette.**"

QUIZ

Name the product or company from the following advertising slogans.

1 Catch the wave.

2 It's gonna be a great day.

3 For skin that looks great... even close up.

4 Get a little closer.

5 Give in to the taste!

6 It's nice to feel so good about a meal.

7 You're gonna love it in an instant.

8 The taste is gonna move ya!

Your dream car at the time was a **Chevrolet Camaro** and your dream job was lead guitarist in Bon Jovi.

You wished your dad was **Jan-Michael Vincent** from *Airwolf*, your mom was **Sigourney Weaver**, and your girlfriend was **Debbie Gibson**.

You used to recite entire episodes of *The Young Ones* at the back of the chemistry lab.

Your collection of mint-condition **Transformers** toys is worth far more now than your endowment mortgage.

The Goonies

Is there another movie that captures a 1980s childhood so perfectly? Contraptions and gadgets, BMX bikes, water chutes, Cyndi Lauper, older brothers in sweats, pirate adventures, skeletons, and a host of weird and wonderful characters. *The Goonies* might just be the all-time greatest kids' movie ever made.

Indiana Jones

You might have been old enough to go to see *Raiders of the Lost Ark* and possibly *The Temple of Doom*. If not, you might have begged your parents to rent *The Last Crusade* on video. In truth, even if you hadn't seen the movies, you knew the name Indiana Jones—and you knew it meant classic swashbuckling action. Though, chances are, you never convinced your parents to buy you a whip.

SHORT CIRCUIT

"Number Five is alive!" Yes, robots were HUGE for 1980s kids. *The Transformers* was kicking serious butt in the cartoon arena, but who could deny the appeal of the strangely E.T.-like Johnny 5, brought to life through another staple of 1980s movie production: practical effects.

YOU KNOW YOU'RE A CHILD OF THE 1980s WHEN...

The name **"George Michael"** makes you think of "Careless Whisper" rather than careless driving.

Your role models were
Gordon Gekko, **Han Solo**,
and **Michael Jordan**.

In 1982, *TIME* magazine
featured a personal computer as
Man of the Year and you were
convinced that **machines** were
poised to take over the world.

Your motto then was "**Girls
Just Want to Have Fun.**"

QUIZ

ONLY A CHILD OF THE 1980s WILL KNOW...

1. Which were the two main locations for the Live Aid mega gig? London and...

2. Which band began their The Wall tour in 1980?

3. *Appetite for Destruction* was the name of which band's first tour (and debut album)?

4. Which former Genesis member participated in the 1988 Human Rights Now! tour, for Amnesty International?

5 Which female artist commenced a top-grossing world tour, called The Moment of Truth Tour, in 1987?

6 Which artist went on a Fun Tour to promote her album *She's So Unusual*?

7 The "Hell's Bell" made its first ever appearance in which hard rock band's tour of 1980–81?

8 Which band opened the Live Aid Wembley show and with which song?

YOU KNOW YOU'RE A CHILD OF THE 1980s WHEN...

You still have your **Pet Monster** in your bedroom.

Partying like it was **1999** once seemed an eternity away.

You can remember when drinking **coffee** wasn't particularly cool, and there were only two types to choose from: black or white.

You wanted to marry **Michael J. Fox** because, at the time, he was the same height as you.

DO YOU REMEMBER...

Guyliner

Guyliner and other make-up can be blamed squarely on the New Romantics, who were very liberal-handed with eyeliner and blusher in particular. Your average disco looked like a casting for a musical.

The Mullet

This legendary yet cringeworthy haircut was really two-in-one: "business in the front, party in the back." There was the spiked mullet, the curly mullet, and the giant fluffy mullet. They were big, but we admit that they weren't clever. Even if George Clooney, Mel Gibson, and Chuck Norris had them, it still doesn't make it right.

THE PERM

Perms were equally as tragic as mullets. It did give you volume—the aim for almost every aspect of women's fashion—but it also kind of made you look as though you'd stuck your fingers in a plug socket. Style icons included Cher, Jon Bon Jovi, and Whitney Houston. And remember not being able to wash your hair for a week afterward so that you didn't pull the curl out? Jeez!

YOU KNOW YOU'RE A CHILD OF THE 1980s WHEN...

You used to say, "By the power of **Grayskull, I am He-Man!**"— and believed it might work.

Your first personal **music player** was about four times the size of this book.

The **Care Bears** and the **Smurfs** were on your Christmas list (and not because you were being ironic).

Jennifer Beals in *Flashdance* was the most erotic thing you'd ever seen, until you discovered that a man did some of her dancing in the movie.

QUIZ

1 Who was the original host of *The Price is Right*?

2 Who was the original host of *Family Feud*?

3 Which *Wheel of Fortune* host died in 1988?

4 Which Nickelodeon show involved ransacking rooms?

5 What did contestants have to collect as they ran through the Fun House?

6 Which early 1980s gameshow focused on video-game-related trivia?

7 Which gameshow involved oversized playing cards?

8 What shape were the spaces on the board in *Blockbusters*?

YOU KNOW YOU'RE A CHILD OF THE 1980s WHEN...

You would rather go barefoot or stomp around in cereal boxes than wear the **sneakers** your **mom** bought you from **Sears**.

You remember laughing at **Steven Wright, Robin Williams,** and **Sam Kinison.**

You had more bleach in your jeans and your hair than **Kim Wilde** and **Billy Idol** combined.

You thought that the most knowledgeable authorities on pop music were **Nina Blackwood, Mark Goodman, Alan Hunter, J.J. Jackson,** and **Martha Quinn.**

DO YOU REMEMBER...

Sony Walkman

Having arrived at the end of the 1970s, a Sony Walkman was the aspirational gadget of the early 1980s. If only the sponge headphones had not been quite so efficient at stripping blusher off every time you wore it.

Disposable Cameras

The Kodak Fling disposable camera was a huge novelty and made front page news when it launched in 1987. At weddings they were often left on tables for guests to snap each other with; no reception was considered worthwhile unless someone snapped the ushers' butts with one of these.

PCs

The first-ever mainstream personal computer, the Macintosh 128K, was originally released as the Apple Macintosh. It came in a beige case with a handy handle on the top for easy transport—who needed a laptop?

Casio Calculator

The Casio-80 calculator watch was surely instrumental in giving geeks a crumb of cool? Being able to do times tables and solve equations while telling the time was quite something back in the 1980s.

Answering machine

Domestic answering machines were such fun! We had to record our own message on a specially designed tape recorder that we linked to our landlines—our only lines back then.

Workmate

Initially rejected by Black & Decker, inventor Ron Hickman rubbed his hands in glee when, in 1981, his Workmate caught on and sold its ten-millionth unit. Ron spotted an international enthusiasm for DIY and created a gadget that no well-dressed shed could do without.

YOU KNOW YOU'RE A CHILD OF THE 1980s WHEN...

Your make-up bag contained an almost limitless supply of **electric-blue** eyeshadow and neon lipstick.

Miss World was essential viewing—and fun for all the family!

You once marveled at the incredible graphics on your **Commodore 64**—they couldn't possibly get more sophisticated than that, could they?

You remember a time when you could hop in the car **without bothering** to buckle your seatbelt and you wouldn't be breaking the law.

QUIZ

ONLY A CHILD OF THE 1980s WILL KNOW...

1 Which Cincinnati Reds manager was banned from baseball for life in 1989?

2 Which boxer was knocked out 91 seconds into a match with Mike Tyson in 1988?

3 Who was the first American gymnast to win the women's all-round gold medal in the 1984 Olympics?

4 Which Cubs manager had an infamous meltdown in 1983?

5 Which tennis player was fined for misconduct at the 1987 US Open?

6 Which golfer won the Masters in 1986 aged 46?

7 Which winner of the 100-meter sprint at the 1988 Olympics had to give up his gold medal because he failed a drug test?

8 Which Olympic gold medalist diver famously cracked his head off the diving board in Seoul in 1988?

YOU KNOW YOU'RE A CHILD OF THE 1980s WHEN...

You remember a time when movies weren't based on old TV series.

You bought a Norwegian phrase book on the off-chance that you might bump into **Morten Harket**.

You slapped your sister during an argument about who was better looking in **CHiPs**: Ponch or Jon.

You used **correction fluid** (and immediately wished you hadn't) to make stripes on your face, just like **Adam Ant**.

Chrysler Minivan

The ultimate family vehicle of the 1980s, Chrysler minivans drove like cars but could fit up to seven passengers. The sliding side door made it easy for you, your siblings, the neighbors, and their dog to pile into the back, and with the seats removed it could double up as a moving van the day your parents packed you off to college.

1961 Ferrari 250GT California Spider

Less than 100 of these were ever made, but that didn't stop us all wanting to get our hands on one of these beauties after watching *Ferris Bueller's Day Off* in 1986.

DELOREAN DMC-12

This futuristic-looking car may not
have had the power and performance
its looks and price tag would suggest,
but it did have those cool gullwing
doors. And it was a freaking
time machine!

YOU KNOW YOU'RE A CHILD OF THE 1980s WHEN...

Your mom let you stay up late just so you could watch the scarier version of the "Thriller" video.

All the new trends—skinny jeans, **Day-Glo** colors and giant headphones—give you a distinct feeling of **déjà vu.**

You had heated debates with friends over **who shot J.R.**

You got your first French kiss at the **school disco** while slow-dancing to Lionel Ritchie and Diana Ross' **"Endless Love."**

QUIZ

ONLY A CHILD OF THE 1980s WILL KNOW...

1 Which famous John was fatally shot in 1980 by a crazed fan?

2 Which writer, actor, and comedian died on July 24, 1980?

3 In which year did Wallis Simpson die?

4 Which famous singer was fatally shot by his father during an argument in their home in 1984?

5 Which Princess and actress died in 1982?

6 Known as the Manassa Mauler, which boxer died in 1983?

7 Which half of the singing duo The Carpenters lost her battle with anorexia in 1983?

8 Which artist and Surrealist icon died in 1989?

YOU KNOW YOU'RE
A CHILD OF THE
1980s
WHEN...

You had nightmares about your face melting after watching *Raiders of the Lost Ark*.

You can sing the chorus
to **"Physical"** by Olivia
Newton-John.

You owned a T-shirt that featured
Toto's tour dates on the back...
or a large **smiley face**
on the front.

You had a mullet to rival
those sported by **Andre
Agassi** and **Jon Bon Jovi.**

"Fresh"

The rise of hip-hop in 1980s pop culture meant that many of the words and phrases that had been used by the artists themselves for years were all of a sudden opened out to the masses. Rap had a unique vocabulary, which seemed infinitely cool to the legions of young fans. "Fresh" had nothing to do with sell-by dates—it meant that something was seriously impressive.

"BAD"

Which is to say "good." Yes, it was confusing to our parents who of course didn't get it, but this twist on linguistic logic was one of the many ways we could make words our own. Suddenly, "bad" became a way to say that something was "dangerously great."

YOU KNOW YOU'RE A CHILD OF THE 1980s WHEN...

Your perfume of choice was **Poison** or **Giorgio Beverly Hills**, and people knew you were coming 20 paces away.

You remember all the names of **Five Star**. (OK, there was Stedman, Lorraine, Delroy, Denise, and Doris.)

You bitterly recall being made to feel a social outcast because you had a **Betamax VCR**.

You thought that "Born in the USA" was the **national anthem.**

QUIZ

ONLY A CHILD OF THE 1980s WILL KNOW...

1. In which country did the Rubik's Cube originate?

2. Which wristwatch fad included interchangeable straps and faces?

3. Dr. Kenneth Cooper was the founder of which 1980s exercise fad?

4. What craze involving specialist footwear was popular in the 1980s?

5 Toru Iwatani created which famous yellow 1980s character?

6 Which toy required balancing and bouncing on a ball at the same time?

7 What kind of bicycle was billed as "the hottest thing on two wheels"?

7 Which colorful card game involved shouting in a different language when you were about to win?

YOU KNOW YOU'RE A CHILD OF THE 1980s WHEN...

No matter what people say, a part of you still believes that a thin leather tie with a piano keyboard printed on it looks cool.

You remember when **FOX**
was still a new TV channel.

Your idea of sophistication was
chicken Kiev accompanied by a
glass of **Beaujolais Nouveau.**

You were off school for two
weeks after dislocating your
shoulder while **breakdancing.**

John McEnroe

This bad boy of tennis was infamous for his outbursts and the immortal words "You cannot be serious!" Despite his on-court behavior, he made it to world number one in 1980 and maintained a series of successes throughout the decade, notably in 1984, when he scored an 82–3 match record that remains the highest single-season win rate of the Open Era.

Michael Jordan

Michael Jordan shot onto the scene in 1986–87, when he scored over 3,000 points in one season. He was also the reason why we all begged our parents for Nike Air Jordan sneakers in 1984.

Hugo Sánchez

Remember the cartwheeling Mexican soccer player? Hugo Sánchez caught the world's attention at the 1986 World Cup by celebrating in athletic style and cartwheeling around the pitch.

Joe Montana

The Comeback Kid started and won four Super Bowls while playing for the San Francisco 49ers. In a game against the Miami Dolphins in 1984, he set the Super Bowl record for most yards passing in a single game (331), prompting coach Bill Walsh to name him "... maybe the greatest quarterback of all time."

Steffi Graf

She had a cool-sounding European name and boy could she play tennis! She achieved a Grand Slam in 1987 and created a huge buzz from commentators and contemporaries alike. Everyone could see she was a star, and she is remembered as one of the all-time greats.

Mike Tyson

Tyson kept viewers hooked as he knocked out champion after champion, remaining undefeated throughout the 1980s. He was the first heavyweight boxer to hold the WBA, WBC and IBF titles at the same time.

YOU KNOW YOU'RE A CHILD OF THE 1980s WHEN...

Your social life used to center around **Trivial Pursuit** and **Pictionary**—or **Twister**, if your parents were cool.

Even today, you wish that your company **car** could talk just like Kitt from *Knight Rider*.

You knew something was supposed to happen when you put on your **Members Only** jacket, you just weren't sure what.

Taking pride of place in your video collection were *Footloose*, *St. Elmo's Fire* and *WarGames*.

QUIZ

Who were the artists or groups who had
hits with the following titles?

1. "Find My Love"

2. "Bette Davis Eyes"

3. "Don't You Want Me?"

4. "Kids in America"

5 "Call Me"

6 "Groovy Kind of Love"

7 "Every Breath You Take"

8 "Private Dancer"

YOU KNOW YOU'RE
A CHILD OF THE
1980s
WHEN...

You were sent to your room
for dancing on the bonnet of
your dad's car à la *Fame*.

Thanks to **Desperately Seeking Susan**, you still have to fight the urge to dry your armpits with a hand dryer.

Your mind was blown by scratch 'n' sniff stickers.

You were savvy enough to know that **Frankie Knuckles** was a Chicago house DJ and not a member of the mafia.

DO YOU REMEMBER...

Tiger Beat

Whether you needed the lowdown on what John Stamos was up to, or wanted some exclusive pics of Rob Lowe on set, *Tiger Beat* was your go-to for gossip and heartthrob pinups.

Bop

Bop's headlines promised to reveal "Why won't Bon Jovi let you down?" and "Has fame changed Johnny Depp?" Plus, there was the "Fly Free To Hollywood" contest, where you had to identify celebs by their eyes or hair alone (not so easy back when everyone who was anyone had a mullet or a perm).

SASSY

Late to the game in the 1980s, only arriving on the scene in 1988, *Sassy* nevertheless made a big impact, with its feminist standpoint and daring to discuss sex education and other topics that the frothier teen mags of the day shied away from.

YOU KNOW YOU'RE A CHILD OF THE 1980s WHEN...

You believed the hype about
Sigue Sigue Sputnik.

You aspired to have the muscles of **B.A. Baracus,** but secretly fancied yourself as the new Face.

You created hundreds of intricate geometric designs with your **Spirograph.** What was the point of them? You weren't exactly sure, but it gave you hours of fun.

You secretly still hoped that 2015 would turn out the way it was in **Back to the Future II.**

QUIZ

ONLY A CHILD OF THE 1980s WILL KNOW...

1 What color did Alice Walker write about?

2 Which Umberto Eco novel was set in Italy in 1327?

3 Who wrote *The Restaurant at the End of the Universe*?

4 Which prolific romantic novelist wrote *Wanderlust*?

5 What kind of verses did Salman Rushdie write?

6 What kind of "crew" did Stephen King write about?

7 *The Fourth Protocol* was written by which popular eighties author? (Clue: initials "F.F.")

8 Who wrote *Hollywood Wives*?

YOU KNOW YOU'RE A CHILD OF THE 1980s WHEN...

You couldn't go to sleep without a bedtime story from **Teddy Ruxpin,** though now the bear's blinking eyes and moving head give you the creeps.

You thought your dad was the bee's knees when he pulled out a **brick-sized phone** at your school sports day.

You hope that Michael J. Fox would go to extreme lengths to get you a **Pepsi**, if you were his new neighbor.

You carried your **ghetto blaster** on your shoulder at the park.

DO YOU REMEMBER...

"Who You Gonna Call?"

If there's one theme song that defined a decade then it was Ray Parker Jr.'s iconic tune for *Ghostbusters*. To this day, no one can resist singing (or shouting) along.

The Hounds of Love

There was something epically fabulous about Kate Bush's fifth studio album and prog rock of a sort. It included the title track, "Cloudbusting," and "Running Up That Hill."

"Hungry Like the Wolf"

Duran Duran had some serious Indiana Jones vibes going on in this music video, and we were there for it. The lyrics were a bit creepy though.

Madonna

With her first album just called *Madonna*, it was pretty clear what she was all about (herself). But it remains a classic 1980s album, with "Lucky Star," "Holiday," and "Borderline" all on there.

Appetite for Destruction

It didn't get much attention when it was first released in 1987, but this album, featuring hits including "Welcome to the Jungle" and "Sweet Child o' Mine" went on to be the bestselling debut album of all time.

Brothers in Arms

In 1985 this was Dire Straits at their most prolific: hit after hit after hit. And we played them into the ground. Again and again.

If you're interested in finding out more
about our books, find us on Facebook at
Summersdale Publishers and follow us on
Twitter at @Summersdale.

www.summersdale.com

IMAGE CREDITS

Cassette tape – pp.5, 9, 13, 17, 21, 25, 29, 33, 37, 41, 45, 49, 53, 57,
61, 65, 69, 73, 77, 81, 85, 89, 93, 97, 101, 105, 109, 113, 117, 121, 125 ©
Mertsaloff/Shutterstock.com; car – pp.5, 9, 13, 17, 21, 25, 29, 33, 37,
41, 45, 49, 53, 57, 61, 65, 69, 73, 77, 81, 85, 89, 93, 97, 101, 105, 113,
109, 113, 121, 125 © Gercen/Shutterstock.com; arcade machine – p.7
© HE6YHIGH/Shutterstock.com; row of media icons – pp.11,19, 27, 35,
43, 51, 59, 67, 75, 83, 91, 99, 107, 115, 123 © SmileStudio/Shutterstock.
com; hip hop graffiti – p.23 © Anton345/Shutterstock.com; workout
– p.39 © UfaBizPhoto/Shutterstock.com; unicorn – p.55 © Svetsol/
Shutterstock.com; Number Five – p.71 © Jose Gil/Shutterstock.
com; woman with perm – p.79 © Mihail Guta/Shutterstock.com;
DeLorean – p.95 © Gercen/Shutterstock.com; 'Who's Bad' – p.103
© Rita Kovács; magazine – p.119 © mileswork/Shutterstock.
com; Rubik's cube – p.128 © Cath Vectorielle/Shutterstock.com